CITIES
OF THE
WORLD

CITIES
OF THE
WORLD

A JOURNEY THROUGH THE MOST FASCINATING CITIES AROUND THE GLOBE

Bath · New York · Singapore · Hong Kong · Cologne · Delhi
Melbourne · Amsterdam · Johannesburg · Auckland · Shenzhen

First published by Parragon in 2011

Parragon
Queen Street House
4 Queen Street
Bath BA1 1HE, UK
www.parragon.com

Designed, produced, and packaged by Stonecastle Graphics Limited

Designed by Sue Pressley and Paul Turner
Text by Philip de Ste. Croix

ISBN 978-1-4454-5655-3

Printed in China

Page one: The imposing outline of the 860-foot (262-m) tall Wisma 46 office tower, the tallest
building in Indonesia, dominates the skyline of downtown Jakarta.

Page two: San Diego sits right on the Pacific shore in southern California. Here, we see the
waterfront skyline of Downtown, which is the city's cultural and financial center.

Page three: One of the most extraordinary cities in the world, Las Vegas is home to the glitz and
glamour of the Strip. The city has been built on the arid desert floor of Clark County, Nevada.
The Strip is lined with an amazing assortment of hotels, casinos, and tourist attractions.

Right: The Space Needle is an iconic element of the Seattle skyline. Opened in 1962, it features
an observation deck at 520 feet (160 m), and below that the rotating SkyCity restaurant.

Contents

Introduction

The city lies at the very heart of the human journey toward civilization. When we look back into prehistory, it is clear that settlement—the act of deliberately living together in built communities—is crucial to our development as a species. The moment when humans stopped operating as small isolated groups of hunters and started to band together into fixed societies is pivotal to the human story. From this developed patterns of agriculture, the exchange of produce, and the beginnings of trade.

It is no coincidence that most of the great cities of the world were established near natural harbors or on major rivers with easy access to the sea, for these were the vital links on the trade routes along which goods could flow most efficiently and profitably. Over time the city grew and gathered to itself a special status. Rich and powerful rulers attracted courts around themselves and the finest artists and craftsmen gravitated toward them; the best educations were to be found in the cities; the structures of government and organized religion were established and maintained in them; and all the while the powerful engine of finance and commerce kept the heart of the city beating to its insistent rhythm.

This strikingly illustrated book showcases the vibrancy and dynamism of cities in the twenty-first century. The variety of cityscapes that we encounter is breathtaking—the Classical elegance of the Parthenon in Athens, for instance, contrasts dramatically with the high-tech modernity of a place such as Shanghai, where new generations of skyscraper are springing up from the earth. In all their many shapes and styles, our cities stand as exciting three-dimensional expressions of the unfailing ingenuity and creativity of the human imagination.

Right: A bird's-eye view looking down at the Pudong district of Shanghai from the immense Shanghai World Financial Center building. The skyscraper dominating the center of the picture is the 88-story Jin Mao tower. Shanghai is quintessentially a modern city—vibrant, bustling with life and enterprise, and constantly reinventing itself to adapt to the fast-changing world of commerce and trade.

Cities of Africa

Casablanca, Morocco

Right: The mosque of Hassan II stands on the shoreline in Casablanca. It was completed in 1993 at the behest of the country's monarch King Hassan II. The minaret is, at 689 feet (210 m), the tallest such mosque tower in the world.

Below: Casablanca is Morocco's largest city as well as its chief port. With a population of around three million people, it is considered the country's economic and business center.

Cairo, Egypt

Above: *The Great Pyramid at Giza and the adjacent Great Sphinx lie about 12 miles (20 km) southwest of Cairo. The pyramid was built in around 2560 BC for the ruler Khufu.*

Top: *Ancient and modern—the Nile River, which has nourished Egyptian civilization for many millennia, sweeps past the modern high-rise cityscape of contemporary Cairo.*

Right: *Begun in 1256, the mosque and madrasa of Sultan Hasan stands in the shadow of the Citadel in Cairo.*

Cape Town, South Africa

Above: *Cape Town's cableway takes visitors on a spectacular aerial ride to the top of Table Mountain above Table Bay.*

Left: *Nestling along the shoreline of the bay, at the northern end of Cape Peninsula, Cape Town is the most popular tourist destination in South Africa. The city is famous for its beautiful natural setting, its harbor, and other well-known landmarks, including Table Mountain and Cape Point. One of the most multicultural cities in the world, it has an estimated population of 3.5 million people.*

Johannesburg, South Africa

Right: *Johannesburg is a major financial center and its skyline reflects the importance of modern commerce—the city contains some of the tallest skyscrapers in Africa.*

Below: *Completed in 1971, the Hillbrow Tower, at 883 feet (269 m) has been the tallest structure in Africa for 40 years. Used for telecommunications, the tower had to be built to a height that would surpass that of the skyscrapers in the city. It is seen here decorated during Johannesburg's hosting of the FIFA Soccer World Cup in 2010.*

Cities of Asia

Jerusalem, Israel

Below: The Christian Quarter of the Old City is a walled area within the boundaries of modern Jerusalem. The domes belong to the Church of the Holy Sepulchre, which is revered as being on the site of Golgotha, where Jesus was crucified.

Left: The Dome of the Rock is located on the Temple Mount in the Old City of Jerusalem. Completed in AD 691, it is the oldest surviving example of early Islamic architecture. The Prophet Muhammad, founder of Islam, is traditionally believed to have ascended into heaven from the site.

Istanbul, Turkey

Above: Istanbul is the world's only metropolis that spans two continents. It is divided by the Bosporus strait—the western portion lies in Europe while the eastern is in Asia. The tall Galata tower was built by Genoese traders in 1348.

Right: The domed basilica of Istanbul's Hagia Sophia, for centuries the city's cathedral, was built under the direction of Emperor Justinian I and was completed in AD 537.

Beijing, China

Right: Beijing has been China's political and cultural center for more than 700 years. As befits a powerhouse economy, the cityscape reflects modernity and prosperity.

Far right: The fifteenth-century Forbidden City comprises the imperial palace complex at the heart of Beijing.

Below: Colloquially nicknamed the Bird's Nest, Beijing's National Stadium was built to host the opening ceremony and the athletics events at the 2008 Summer Olympics.

Hong Kong, China

Right: Meaning "Fragrant Harbor" in Cantonese, Hong Kong has been an important trading center since the nineteenth century, when it became a British crown colony. Tourist junks still ply the waters between the Island and Kowloon.

Below: Gloucester Road is an important thoroughfare that runs through the heart of Hong Kong Island's commercial and financial center parallel to the harbor front. It connects to the Cross-Harbour Tunnel, which takes traffic to Kowloon.

Below: One of the greatest nighttime cityscapes in the world—the view from Victoria Peak in Hong Kong looking down at the vibrant center of Hong Kong Island itself, the harbor beyond, and the lights of Kowloon on the Chinese mainland in the distance. The tallest building is Two International Finance Centre (or 2 IFC as it is more commonly known). Completed in 2003 and designed to provide office accommodation for numerous prestigious financial institutions, it stands an impressive 1,362 feet (415 m) tall. It was Hong Kong's tallest tower until it was overtopped in 2010 by the International Commerce Center in Kowloon.

Shanghai, China

Right: The Pudong district skyline at night. The most prominent building, lit up on the left, is the Oriental Pearl Tower. It is principally a TV tower, but it also contains a hotel, restaurant, and observation platforms. To the right are the Jin Mao tower and the taller Shanghai World Financial Center.

Below: Situated at the mouth of the Yangtze River, Shanghai has long enjoyed a reputation as a crossroads of trade between east and west. It is China's most populous city and is well on the way to becoming a major global financial center.

Above: Shanghai is not just about gleaming twenty-first-century thrust and glamour; older traditional pagoda styles of Chinese architecture still find a place in the city.

Opposite: An aerial view of Shanghai's Bund and Pudong districts lit up at night. The tallest building is the Shanghai World Financial Center, which at 1,614 feet (492 m) high is the tallest skyscraper in mainland China and the third tallest in the world. In front of it is the Jin Mao tower, the home of the five-star, 555-room Shanghai Grand Hyatt hotel which occupies floors 53 to 87. The lower floors are offices.

Tokyo, Japan

Right: The Rainbow Bridge is a suspension bridge crossing Tokyo Bay. The supporting towers are white in color, but at night they are illuminated with colored lights using solar energy obtained during the day.

Below: Tokyo has grown from being a humble fishing village on the coast of Honshu island to its current position as one of the world's top three financial "command centers." Tokyo is home to over 12 million people and an additional 3 million people come into the city each day to work.

Dubai, United Arab Emirates

Above: Jumeirah is a coastal residential area that has become
one of the most sought-after addresses in Dubai.

Right: The iconic Burj Al Arab hotel in Dubai is the fourth tallest
hotel in the world and was designed to resemble the sail of a
ship. It stands 1,053 feet (321 m) tall and is constructed on an
artificial island 920 feet (280 m) from Jumeirah beach, where it is
connected to the mainland by a curving bridge.

Kolkata, India

Right: The Victoria Memorial Hall was designed as a permanent memorial to the British presence in India and the memory of Queen Victoria. Combining elements of European and Mughal building styles, it was the work of British architect Sir William Emerson and was completed in 1921.

Below: Howrah district lies just across the Hooghly River from Kolkata in West Bengal. Here, shoppers congregate in a bustling roadside market, where they can buy flowers to use in religious ceremonies and to mark family celebrations.

Mumbai, India

Above: The largest city in India, Mumbai has long been metaphorically known as the Gateway to India. In 1911, a ceremonial gateway of the same name was erected to celebrate the first visit to India by a British king and queen. Fittingly, the last British viceroy left India through this gateway in 1947, when India gained her independence.

Left: This splendid neo-Gothic edifice is Victoria Terminus, now known as Chhatrapati Shivaji Terminus (CST). Opened in 1887, it is one of the busiest railroad stations in India.

Bangkok, Thailand

Above: Beautifully illuminated in the purple evening light, one of the iconic sights of Bangkok, the Wat Arun, or Temple of the Dawn, rises majestically above the Thonburi west bank of the Chao Phraya River. The central tower, or prang, is built in Khmer style and represents Mount Meru, a sacred mountain in Buddhist and Hindu cosmology. It is topped with a seven-pronged trident. The four smaller prangs symbolize the four winds. Building work on the temple was started by King Rama II in the early part of the nineteenth century, and it was completed by his successor Rama III.

Right: Originally a small trading post on the west bank of the lower Chao Phraya River, Bangkok became the capital of Thailand in 1768. It is now the largest urban area in the country and its economic center. Despite rapid modernization, the city has retained its historic landmarks, which attract some 10 million international visitors each year.

Singapore, Republic of Singapore

Above: A panorama of the bay on which Singapore is situated. The incredible buildings on the left are the three 55-story towers of the Marina Bay Sands hotel. On top sits the SkyPark, which includes landscaped gardens, an infinity swimming pool, an observation deck, and restaurants.

Right: The merlion is an official symbol of Singapore and this statue was unveiled by Prime Minister Lee Kuan Yew in 1972. It used to stand at the mouth of the Singapore River but has been relocated to Merlion Park fronting Marina Bay.

Cities of Europe

Moscow, Russia

Left: *Saint Basil's Cathedral in Red Square is one of the best-known landmarks to which tourists flock while in Russia. It marks the very center of Moscow. A Russian Orthodox cathedral, the building was constructed between 1555–61 on the orders of Czar Ivan IV (the Terrible) to commemorate a military victory. The extraordinary colors applied to the walls and onion domes mainly date from the seventeenth century, when the building was refurbished.*

Above: *Red Square is a large rectangular plaza that was once an open-air market and the venue for the great May Day military parades of the Soviet era. Many people now come to visit the Lenin Mausoleum, where the embalmed body of the celebrated Soviet leader is displayed, and the Kremlin.*

Opposite: *The Friendship of Nations Fountain stands outside the All-Russian Exhibition Center, founded in 1939 as the site for an agricultural exhibition in Moscow. It features gilded statues of maidens in the national costumes of the 16 Soviet Republics surrounding a golden sheaf of wheat.*

Warsaw, Poland

Above: The mermaid, or syrenka, is the symbol of Warsaw, and it can be found on statues throughout the city and on the civic coat of arms. This bronze is a cast of a statue made in 1855 by Konstanty Hegel and it can be found in the Old Town.

Right: The Castle Square in Warsaw with the Royal Castle just visible on the right and St. John's Cathedral and the Old Town in the center. This part of the city was leveled by the German army in 1944 during the Warsaw Uprising, but it has been carefully reconstructed in the postwar period.

Prague, Czech Republic

Above: The Charles Bridge (the second bridge in the picture) is a famous Prague landmark. The balustrades are decorated with statues of 30 saints that were mostly erected between 1683 and 1714. The Old Town bridge tower (lit up) is considered a particularly fine example of civic Gothic architecture.

Left: Prague is situated on the Vltava River in central Bohemia. It is an ancient city and for centuries was the permanent seat of two Holy Roman emperors and, thus, was also the capital of the Holy Roman Empire.

Reykjavík, Iceland

Above: Located on the southern shore of Faxaflói Bay in southwestern Iceland, Reykjavík is the northernmost capital of a sovereign state. It is a major fishing port and the commercial, financial, and administrative center of Iceland.

Left: The Hallgrímskirkja is the largest church in Iceland. It took 38 years to build, construction work beginning in 1945 and ending in 1986. The landmark tower stands 244 feet (74.5 m) tall. The statue in front is a memorial to Leif Eriksson, a Norse explorer who is thought to have been the first European to land in North America in the eleventh century.

Helsinki, Finland

Above: A fine panorama of Helsinki that lies in the very south of
Finland on a peninsula that juts out into the Gulf of Finland.
It was founded in 1550 by King Gustav I Vasa of Sweden, but was
repeatedly damaged and burned over the following centuries.
The present city mainly dates from the nineteenth century. The
large white building is Helsinki Cathedral, a neoclassical church
dating from 1830–52. It was designed by German architect Carl
Ludvig Engel, who was also responsible for rebuilding much of
the center when it was still under Russian rule.

Vienna, Austria

Above: This panorama of Vienna was photographed from the Wiener Riesenrad, the giant Ferris wheel that stands at the entrance to the Prater amusement park. The city sits on the banks of the Danube, Europe's second-longest river.

Right: The Belvedere consists of two Baroque palaces that stand at either end of a terraced garden. It was built in the early eighteenth century as a summer residence for Prince Eugene of Savoy. The chief architect was Johann Lukas von Hildebrandt. The photograph shows the Upper Belvedere.

Berlin, Germany

Above: Berliner Dom, or Berlin Cathedral, dates from 1905 but stands on the site of several earlier houses of worship.

Above right: One of the most instantly recognizable landmarks in Europe—the Brandenburg Gate in central Berlin. During the Cold War it stood at the divide between East and West Berlin, but in 1989 it came to symbolize German reunification.

Right: The Norman Foster-designed glass dome that now sits on top of the Reichstag parliament building in Berlin.

Zurich, Switzerland

Right: Zurich, the largest city in Switzerland, lies in the center
of the country at the northwestern end of Lake Zurich. In this
picture, we see the Limmat, one of two rivers that run through
the city. The church on the left is St. Peter, parts of which date
to the thirteenth century—the clock face measures 28 1/2 feet
(8.7 m) in diameter, the largest in Europe.

Below: Zurich boasts an elegant and well preserved old town,
the Altstadt, which approximately corresponds to the area
enclosed by the former city ramparts.

Stockholm, Sweden

Above: Stockholm is sometimes poetically referred to as the
Venice of the north because so much of the city is built next to
water. In fact, it stands on a group of 14 islands located on the
southeast coast of Sweden at the mouth of Lake Mälaren. This
view shows (on the right) Riddarholmen Church on the island of
Riddarholmen, which is where many Swedish monarchs are
buried. The white circular building in the foreground is Birger Jarls
Torn, a sixteenth-century fortified tower built by King Gustav I
Vasa as a defensive measure. In the background is Gamla Stan,
the old town.

Paris, France

Right: The brainchild of French engineer Gustave Eiffel, the 984-feet (300-m) tall Eiffel Tower opened the 1889 World Exhibition in Paris. Intended to stand for 20 years, tourists loved it so much that it was not demolished as planned, and it has become one of the most famous landmarks in the world.

Below: The Louvre, a French royal palace of long standing, was first used as a museum in 1793. In the 1980s a 69-feet (21-m) tall glass pyramid was added to the museum's courtyard to serve as an entrance to the world-famous exhibition spaces.

Opposite: Famous as the domain of the fictional hunchback bellringer Quasimodo, here a gargoyle on the roof of Notre Dame Cathedral looks out over Paris. The Basilica of the Sacré Coeur, seen on the summit of Montmartre Hill in the distance (the highest point in the city), dominates the surrounding district. It was completed in 1919 and paid for by national subscription. Montmartre is famous for its nightclubs and association with celebrated artists, including Picasso, van Gogh, Modigliani, Dali, and Toulouse-Lautrec. Notre Dame itself is situated on Ile de la Cité in the middle of the Seine River and is one of the most famous Gothic cathedrals in the world.

Amsterdam, The Netherlands

Right: Amsterdam is a city built around water. Its name derives from Amstellerdam, a reference to the damming of the Amstel River which led to the foundation of the first settlement in the thirteenth century.

Below: The inner part of the city is divided into "islands" by concentric rings of canals that are crisscrossed by a network of more than 1,000 bridges. Amsterdam lacks big open spaces, but it does have a wonderful sense of intimacy with beautifully gabled houses cluster together on the banks of the canals.

Brussels, Belgium

Above: The central square in Brussels, the Grande Place, is ringed by imposing guild halls and the city's town hall. It has been designated a UNESCO World Heritage Site.

Right: Situated close to the Grande Place, rue des Bouchers is a picturesque cobbled street that is crammed with restaurants vying to attract hungry passers-by to their tables.

Edinburgh, Scotland

Above: Edinburgh's dramatic setting and impressive examples of architecture dating back centuries make it one of the most picturesque cities in Europe. This is the view over the city from the top of Calton Hill, where this memorial to the philosopher Dugald Stewart was erected in 1831.

Right: Scotland's most visited tourist attraction, Edinburgh Castle, perches on Castle Rock high above the city. Most of the fortifications date to the sixteenth century but the oldest building, St. Margaret's Chapel, is early twelfth century.

Dublin, Ireland

Left: The fine neoclassical facade of the Custom House which stands on the north bank of the River Liffey. Designed by James Gandon as a collection center for customs dues levied by the port of Dublin, it was opened in 1791.

Right: This statue of a former Provost, George Salmon, stands outside Trinity College, Dublin, in Parliament Square.

Below: The Ha'penny Bridge over the Liffey dates from 1816. Made of cast iron, the bridge was fabricated in Shropshire, England.

London, England

Right: *The Thames River has been central to the history of London from as long ago as the time of Roman occupation of Britain. In this view, looking upstream, we see the London Eye in front of County Hall on the left, and the Houses of Parliament and Big Ben lit up on the right bank.*

Below: *One of the most instantly recognizable landmarks in the world, Tower Bridge was opened in 1894. The design allows for the two sections of the lower bridge to be raised to allow for the passage of tall-masted ships to the Pool of London.*

Right: *Another iconic symbol of London, the Royal Albert Hall in South Kensington was designed as a memorial to Prince Albert, the husband of Queen Victoria, and was built between 1867 and 1871. It hosts concerts, most notably the Proms music season every summer, and sporting events.*

Opposite below right: *Quintessential London—a Grenadier Guardsman in scarlet tunic and bearskin on sentry duty outside Buckingham Palace. The ceremony of Changing The Guard takes place at 11 a.m. on the Palace forecourt when the keys of the Palace are ceremonially handed to the new guard.*

Below: *The world's great cities are not preserved in aspic as mere museum pieces; they continually reinvent themselves in response to the new generations of people who live in them and the dynamism of their business and cultural lives. This view of the skyline of the City of London with Blackfriars Bridge in the foreground is clear evidence of that. Next to Sir Christopher Wren's masterpiece, St. Paul's Cathedral, can be seen the cranes that are toiling to create the modern high-rise city skyline. The distinctive curved building on the right is the Norman Foster-designed "Gherkin," 30 St. Mary Axe.*

Rome, Italy

Above: The Colosseum is unusual among ancient Roman amphitheaters in that it is totally freestanding instead of being partially excavated from a hillside. Completed in AD 80, it was dedicated by Emperor Titus in a ceremony that included 100 days of gladiatorial contests and displays.

Left: The majestic Trevi Fountain is a late Roman Baroque masterpiece designed by Nicola Salvi. It was completed in 1762. Tradition holds that any visitor who throws a coin into the fountain is destined to return to Rome.

Venice, Italy

Above: *The Grand Canal is Venice's main waterway that divides the city in two. It traces an S-shape course stretching from St. Mark's Basilica in the east to the lagoon near Santa Lucia Grandi railroad terminus in the west. The buildings lining the canal include luxurious palazzi that were owned by the noblest Venetian families. They range in date from the thirteenth to the eighteenth centuries and encompass many architectural styles including Byzantine, Gothic, Renaissance, Baroque, and neoclassical.*

Left: *One of four bridges spanning the Grand Canal, the famous Rialto Bridge is the oldest bridge across the canal. Designed by Antonio da Ponte, the single-span stone construction was completed in 1591 and has become an iconic image of Venice.*

Barcelona, Spain

Left: One of the most extraordinary buildings in the world, the church of the Holy Family (Sagrada Família) was begun by architect Antoni Gaudí in 1883, and it occupied the rest of his life. It is still unfinished but building work continues.

Below: Barcelona is built right next to the sea on the coast of Catalonia. It is Spain's largest port and second largest city. This is the view looking northeast toward the old part of the city. The low building in the foreground is the Maritime Museum with the pillar monument to Christopher Columbus on the right.

Athens, Greece

Above: The Acropolis occupies a rocky hill overlooking Athens. It was built in the second half of the fifth century BC to the glory of the goddess Athena. The main building seen here is the Parthenon, a temple to Athena, constructed under the direction of the statesman Pericles. It has lost most of its sculpture, but the underlying marble structure is intact.

Right: The view looking down from the Acropolis. Modern Athens is a young city—the construction boom began in the 1950s to keep pace with a population explosion.

Cities of Central & South America

Mexico City, Mexico

Right: The business district of Mexico City. Skyscrapers line Paseo de la Reforma, a boulevard that cuts diagonally across the city. Torre Mayor, at 738 feet (225 m) one of the highest skyscrapers in Latin America, is on the right.

Above: The Palacio de Bellas Artes in Mexico City is the country's principal center for fine arts. It was built in the 1930s under the direction of Mexican architect Federico Mariscal and includes famous murals by Diego Rivera.

Buenos Aires, Argentina

Above: The birthplace of tango, Buenos Aires is a city rich with culture and vibrancy. It lies on the western shore of the estuary of the Río de la Plata, and its architecture is an eclectic mix of European and South American styles with a healthy dash of modern high-rise added for good measure.

Left: An emblem of Buenos Aires, the Casa Rosada (Pink House) is the seat of government and houses the offices of Argentina's president. Its architecture is Beaux Arts, an elaborate style popular in the nineteenth century.

Rio de Janeiro, Brazil

Right: *The statue of Christ the Redeemer stands on the summit of Corcovado Hill overlooking Rio de Janeiro. Constructed of soapstone and reinforced concrete and measuring 130 feet (39.6 m) in height, it was sculpted by French sculptor Paul Landowski and was completed in 1931.*

Opposite: *One of the most famous and fashionable beaches in the world, Copacabana is a 2 ½ -mile (4-km) stretch of sand that is situated in the southern part of Rio de Janeiro.*

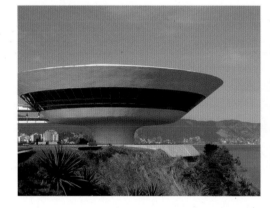

Above: *The Niteról Contemporary Art Museum is one of Rio de Janeiro's main landmarks. Said to resemble a UFO (unidentified flying object), this modernist saucer-shape structure was completed in 1996. It projects over a large reflecting pool, and visitors can enjoy beautiful views of the city, Guanabara Bay, and Sugarloaf Mountain from its viewing gallery.*

Cities of North America

Toronto, Canada

Right: Gleaming against the evening sky, Toronto's CN Tower dwarfs everything around it. It stands an amazing 1,815 feet (553.3 m) tall and was completed in 1976.

Below: Toronto lies on the northern shores of Lake Ontario. It was founded in 1793 as York by American colonists loyal to the British, and it received its current name in 1834. It is the largest city in Canada, with more than 2.5 million residents.

Vancouver, Canada

Above: The slopes of the North Shore Mountains form Vancouver's distinctive backdrop. It was the host city for the 2010 Winter Olympics and the Paralympic Games.

Left: The geodesic dome is the location of Science World, a science center hosting interactive displays and exhibits.

Right: Vancouver is a young city. In 1867, it was the site of a logging sawmill, but the arrival of the railroad in 1887 saw the port rapidly increase in size and national importance.

Chicago, Illinois

Above: Oak Street Beach is found adjacent to Lake Shore Drive, where Chicago fronts onto the western side of Lake Michigan. It is one of Chicago's most popular lakeshore recreation spots and attracts fitness enthusiasts, sunbathers, and swimmers.

Above right: Downtown Chicago at night with the Aon Center (tallest building). Chicago was founded in 1833, and has grown into the third most populous U.S. city and a major financial and commercial center. The skyline here is among the world's tallest and most densely packed with skyscrapers.

Right: Millennium Park is a public park near the shoreline which opened in 2004. Its centerpiece is this sculpture called Cloud Gate by British artist Anish Kapoor. Characteristically it uses large, polished, curved surfaces to reflect and distort the viewer's vision of the sky and surrounding cityscape.

Boston, Massachusetts

Above: The statue of Paul Revere in front of Old North Church commemorates his midnight ride from Boston to Lexington in 1775 to warn of British troop movements.

Above left: Founded in 1630 by Puritans from England, Boston is one of America's oldest cities. It developed into a major shipping port, commercial center, and tourist destination.

Left: Beacon Hill is a historic part of Boston that is famous for its picturesque narrow cobbled streets and gas lamps.

New York, New York

Right: Times Square is a major commercial intersection in the borough of Manhattan, at the junction of Broadway and Seventh Avenue. Nicknamed "The Crossroads of the World," it is a popular attraction for tourists visiting the city.

Below: The Flatiron Building, so called because of its unusual wedge shape, is located at 175 Fifth Avenue, Manhattan. Completed in 1902 and standing 285 feet (86 m) tall, it is considered to be one of the first skyscrapers ever built. It was an immediate success with local New Yorkers.

Left: The New York Stock Exchange is located at 11 Wall Street in lower Manhattan. The largest stock exchange in the world, its origins can be traced back to 1792, when an agreement was signed by 24 stockbrokers under a buttonwood tree on Wall Street, where they habitually gathered.

Opposite: The Statue of Liberty was designed by French sculptor Frédéric-Auguste Bartholdi and was presented as a gift to the United States from the people of France in 1886. The sculpture on Liberty Island in New York Harbor has become an iconic symbol of freedom and of the United States.

Washington D. C.

Right: One of the great sights in Washington D. C., the United States Capitol, where the U. S. Congress convenes, is located on Capitol Hill. Designed by William Thornton, remarkably, a doctor with no formal architectural training, the cornerstone of the building was laid by President George Washington in 1793.

Below: The Washington Monument was built to honor America's first president. Building work was halted by the American Civil War and, when resumed, the color of the marble used in the top section differed slightly from that of the base.

San Francisco, California

Above: One of the most instantly recognizable structures in the world, the Golden Gate Bridge spans San Francisco Bay and connects the city to Marin County to the north. It was opened in 1937; the main span is 4,200 feet (1,280 m) long.

Right: One of San Francisco's iconic cable cars climbs away from Fisherman's Wharf up a steep incline. The system works by means of constantly moving cables that the cars can either grip (to move) or release (to slow down and stop), using a lever that is operated by a highly skilled gripman.

New Orleans, Louisiana

Above: Jackson Square is right in the middle of the French Quarter. In the background is St. Louis Cathedral, while the statue commemorates General Andrew Jackson (1747–1845).

Left: New Orleans is renowned as being the birthplace of jazz and music remains a significant part of life on the street.

Right: New Orleans was founded in 1718 by a Frenchman but was sold to the United States by Napoleon in 1803. Its distinctive French Quarter is the most historic part of the city.

Los Angeles, California

Left: The magic of Hollywood adds a very special sprinkling of stardust to LA. Hollywood produces about half of the feature movies shot in the United States and the industry contributes tens of millions of dollars to the city's economy.

Below: A glittering evening cityscape showcases the bright lights of Los Angeles, the second largest city in the United States. Established in 1771 as a Spanish mission, the modern city stretches across a wide coastal plain in California between various ranges of mountains and the Pacific Ocean.

Cities of Oceania

Sydney, Australia

Opposite: Unmistakably Sydney! The Sydney Opera House, which resembles a number of sail-like shell forms, was designed by Danish architect Jørn Utzon in 1957. Construction was difficult, partly because of the revolutionary design, and the opera house only opened in 1973. Behind it stands Sydney Harbour Bridge, another instantly recognizable landmark. Nicknamed the "Coat Hanger" by local Sydney residents, it opened in March 1932 and carries rail, road, and foot traffic.

Above: The Metro Monorail runs on a loop that serves eight stations around the center of the city. The tall building in the background is Sydney Tower, an observation tower that stands 1,014 feet (309 m) tall, including the spire. Visitors can access the Skywalk, a glass-floored platform near the top.

Right: Remarkably, Sydney was founded as a penal colony back in 1788, but it has grown in the past two centuries to establish itself as Australia's largest and most important city. Its superb natural harbor, Port Jackson, means that it is also one of the most thriving ports on the Pacific seaboard.

Melbourne, Australia

Left: Federation Square is a recent addition to the Melbourne landscape, a public space that has become one of the city's central hubs. It features museums, cafes, and a stage and giant screen that hosts concerts and shows sporting events.

Below: Melbourne is located on the large natural bay known as Port Phillip on the southeastern coast of Australia, with the city center positioned at the estuary of the Yarra River (at the northernmost point of the bay). It is a lively metropolis and is sometimes called "the cultural capital" of Australia.

Above: Melbourne's Coops Shot Tower comprises a Victorian-era tower (designed for the production of shot balls by freefall of molten lead) that has been encased inside a 262-foot (80-m) tall conical glass roof as part of Melbourne Central, a hub containing shops, offices, and a railroad station.

Auckland, New Zealand

Above: The deep channels and small tides found at Waitemata Harbour have led to it becoming New Zealand's most important port. This view across the water from Devenport shows the city's modern skyline dominated by Sky Tower, an observation and telecommunications tower that stands 1,076 feet (328 m) tall. The upper section contains a revolving restaurant that makes one full revolution every hour.

Left: Auckland lies in the northwestern part of the North Island, on an isthmus between Waitemata and Manukau harbors. The largest city and commercial center in New Zealand, Auckland is home to many cultures and is considered to be the center for visual arts in New Zealand.

Index

Picture Credits

a = above, b = below, r = right, l = left, c = center

© shutterstock.com: 18b, 23a; Henrik Winther Andersen 57a; Boguslaw Bafia 40br; Jill Battaglia 52ar; Stuart Berman 53al; S.Borisov 43a, 45a; BestPhoto1 26r; Tomasz Bidermann 26al; Ruth Black 19l; Lori Monahan Borden 58br; Boykov 52br; Dan Breckwoldt 35; Joseph Calev 4–5, 19r; Ana del Castillo 37a; Jo Chambers 61r; Hung Chung Chih 20bl; clearlens 30br; courtyardpix 27a; Neale Cousland 23b, 62ar; Cameron Cross 58bl; Songquan Deng 54bl; devi 36b; dibrova 40bl; Dubova 12b; Eastimages 14b; Elena Elisseeva 50b; Helen & Vlad Filatov 24r; Frontpage 46r; gary718 54bc; godrick 38bc; Warren Goldswain 1; Maksym Gorpenyuk 13b; Lijuan Guo 51br; Sergio Hayashi 46cl; Lukas Hlavac 21br; Inhabitant 25; Invisible 62al; Andrey Jitkov 24l; Brian K. 9a, 42l; karnizz 31al; Korobanova 11r; Jan Kratochvila 60; emin kuliyev 54ar; Chee-Onn Leong 53bl; leungchopan 15a, 15br; Pius Lee 9cl; rj lerich 8cl; Mikhail Levit 12a; Giancarlo Liguori 48l; Thierry Maffeis 39b; Cosmin Manci 45b; Russell Marini 50ac; Oleksiy Mark 29, 33; Andriy Markov 30a; Rafael Martin-Gaitero 47a; MC_PP 18a; Merlindo 38a; Lazar Mihai-Bogdan 34l; momorad 62bl; Tatiana Morozova 62b; Luciano Mortula 22r, 43b; Ulrich Mueller 32l; Mikhail Nekrasov 9br; ndrpggr 34r; Walid Nohra 27bl; olly 16bl; Mark Van Overmeire 10l; paparazzit 31ar; Losevsky Pavel 39al; Marc Pinter 31bc; Chris Pole 28b; posztos (colorlab.hu) 8r; Celso Pupo 49; QQ7 40a; Walter Quirtmair 61cl; rarena 58a; Paul Reid 31ar; RDM Photo 44a; Jeremy Richards 20r; Eduardo Rivero 47b; r.nagy 41a; David Ryznar 10r; Jorge Salcedo 53r; Chris Sargent 41b; Sarunyu_foto 22al; Mark Schwettmann 48l; SFC 56r; sjeacle 39ar; Luke Schmidt 11bl; Michael Sobers 52al; Dmitry Sokolov 44b; ssguy 6–7, 17; Nickolay Stanev 21a; Ronald Sumners 32r; Sunshinepig 16a; Albert H. Teich 63a; Christophe Testi 57bc; testing 14ac; Vitaly Titov & Maria Sidelnikova 36a; trekandshoot 59al; tungtopgun 42r; Tupungato 37bc; upthebanner 55; urmoments 56bl; Ivo Vitanov Velinov 13a; Ian D Walker 14ar; Xuanlu Wang 51bl; Paul Yates 51a; Andy Z. 2, 3, 59b; claudio zaccherini 15bl, 16cr.

© istockphoto.com: Stephan Hoerold 28a.